The gospel in all of life

2 Corinthians

by Gary Millar

thegoodbook
COMPANY

2 Corinthians For You

If you are reading *2 Corinthians For You* alongside this Good Book Guide, here is how the studies in this booklet link to the chapters of *2 Corinthians For You*:

Study One → Ch 1-2   Study Five → Ch 8
Study Two → Ch 3-4   Study Six → Ch 9-10
Study Three → Ch 5   Study Seven → Ch 10-11
Study Four → Ch 6-7

Find out more about *2 Corinthians For You* at:
www.thegoodbook.com/for-you

The gospel in all of life
The Good Book Guide to 2 Corinthians
© Gary Millar/The Good Book Company, 2020
Series Consultants: Tim Chester, Tim Thornborough,
                    Anne Woodcock, Carl Laferton

Published by:
The Good Book Company

thegoodbook.com | thegoodbook.co.uk
thegoodbook.com.au | thegoodbook.co.nz | thegoodbook.co.in

ISBN: 9781784983895

Printed in Turkey

CONTENTS

Introduction: Good Book Guides

Every Bible-study group is different—yours may take place in a church building, in a home or in a cafe, on a train, over a leisurely mid-morning coffee or squashed into a 30-minute lunch break. Your group may include new Christians, mature Christians, non-Christians, mums and tots, students, businessmen or teens. That's why we've designed these *Good Book Guides* to be flexible for use in many different situations.

Our aim in each session is to uncover the meaning of a passage, and see how it fits into the "big picture" of the Bible. But that can never be the end. We also need to appropriately apply what we have discovered to our lives. Let's take a look at what is included:

⊕ **Talkabout:** Most groups need to "break the ice" at the beginning of a session, and here's the question that will do that. It's designed to get people talking around a subject that will be covered in the course of the Bible study.

⊕ **Investigate:** The Bible text for each session is broken up into manageable chunks, with questions that aim to help you understand what the passage is about. The **Leader's Guide** contains **guidance for questions**, and sometimes ⊗ additional "follow-up" questions.

⊡ **Explore more (optional):** These questions will help you connect what you have learned to other parts of the Bible, so you can begin to fit it all together like a jig-saw; or occasionally look at a part of the passage that's not dealt with in detail in the main study.

⊕ **Apply:** As you go through a Bible study, you'll keep coming across **apply** sections. These are questions to get the group discussing what the Bible teaching means in practice for you and your church. ⊡ **Getting personal** is an opportunity for you to think, plan and pray about the changes that you personally may need to make as a result of what you have learned.

⊕ **Pray:** We want to encourage prayer that is rooted in God's word—in line with his concerns, purposes and promises. So each session ends with an opportunity to review the truths and challenges highlighted by the Bible study, and turn them into prayers of request and thanksgiving.

The **Leader's Guide** and introduction provide historical background information, explanations of the Bible texts for each session, ideas for **optional extra** activities, and guidance on how best to help people uncover the truths of God's word.

Why study 2 Corinthians?

Corinth was the ancient world's equivalent of a modern, thriving, multicultural city. When Paul showed up in Corinth for the first time, he found a city with a Roman face, a Greek heart, a large Jewish minority and a deeply ingrained universal desire to impress. It's hardly a shock then that, when Paul preached the gospel and a church was born, life got pretty complicated. What else would you expect from a bunch of people who are mostly Greek following a suffering and dying Jewish Messiah in the middle of a Roman city which prides itself on always coming out on top. Welcome to the mess that is Corinth.

Now I know that church is always messy. I know that ministry is always more complicated than we first think. But it's also true that some places are more messy than others. And Corinth was one of those places. And Paul's relationship with the messy church he had planted in this complex city was... yes, you guessed it, *messy*.

Paul had a difficult relationship with the church he had planted. After he left, he had to write them numerous letters, some of them now lost. In them, he teaches, he rebukes, he reminds them of the basics that they had so quickly forgotten about. And then he had what he describes in 2 Corinthians 1 as "the painful visit". And at this point in their relationship, it's still not entirely clear whether the church will flourish and grow or crash and burn—which explains why this is the most passionate, honest, vulnerable, heartfelt letter in the Bible. The battle for hearts and minds is still on in Corinth. In particular, the leaders that Paul left behind continue to waver. So Paul writes in an attempt to persuade them to stick with him and the gospel.

That's why I think this letter is the place to go in the New Testament for a description and embodiment of what gospel ministry is all about. For Paul, gospel ministry is what we all do. It is walking with, speaking for, and serving Jesus in all of life. This letter is written for all of us. 2 Corinthians takes us through how to live by faith in our broken world. It's the key to embracing our weakness and living in the strength which God himself supplies.

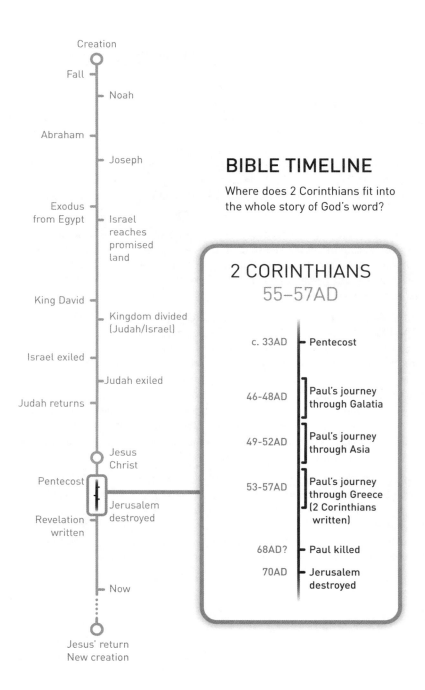

BIBLE TIMELINE

Where does 2 Corinthians fit into the whole story of God's word?

Creation
Fall
Noah
Abraham
Joseph
Exodus from Egypt
Israel reaches promised land
King David
Kingdom divided (Judah/Israel)
Israel exiled
Judah exiled
Judah returns
Jesus Christ
Pentecost
Jerusalem destroyed
Revelation written
Now
Jesus' return
New creation

2 CORINTHIANS
55–57AD

c. 33AD — Pentecost

46-48AD — Paul's journey through Galatia

49-52AD — Paul's journey through Asia

53-57AD — Paul's journey through Greece (2 Corinthians written)

68AD? — Paul killed

70AD — Jerusalem destroyed

1

2 Corinthians 1 – 2

BEGINNING WITH GOD

⊕ talkabout

1. Why do you think church can be such a messy and difficult environment for people? What common problems can destroy a church if they are left unaddressed?

⊕ investigate

Paul is writing to a messy church with many problems in its leadership. In this passionate letter he is appealing to them to stick with him, and with the gospel message.

▶ Read 2 Corinthians 1:1-2

2. What do the opening two verses suggest are some of the issues that need to be addressed in Corinth?

3. Grace and peace are the twin marks of the local church, according to Paul. How does the gospel produce these key qualities?

⊡ getting personal

Have you grasped the fact that the church belongs to God (v 1)?
Is that reflected in the way you speak about church; care about
church; treat your brothers and sisters?

⊕ investigate

> **❯ Read 2 Corinthians 1:3-11**

4. Who comforts whom in these verses? And why do they need to be
comforted?

• What aspects of God's character does Paul highlight here?

• How should our view of God and suffering change in light of these truths?

➔ apply

5. What is the worst thing you have ever suffered? Did you experience the
love and comfort of God as you were going through it?

- How are we able to show the love and comfort of God to others who are in distressing circumstances?

⊡ getting personal

Are you fearful about what may happen to you in the future—for example, your job and career, where you will live, finding a partner, your care in later life, or if you become house-bound or have dementia? How will you exercise your trust in God for the future and what it may contain for you? How might you use one or more of these verses to encourage someone who is currently going through trials?

⊡ explore more

optional

❯ Read 2 Corinthians 1:12 – 2:11

Why does Paul write so much to them about how his travel plans had changed, do you think?

What comes out of this section about how trustworthy and accountable Christian leaders should be?

⊡ investigate

❯ Read 2 Corinthians 2:12-17

Paul compares his life and work to a Roman triumphal procession, where the defeated captives are being led by the victor with incense burners.

6. Who leads this procession and what is the aroma they spread?

DICTIONARY

Troas (v 12): see map on page 69.
Gospel (v 12): Greek word meaning "good news". The gospel is the good news about Jesus Christ.

7. How do different groups respond to the smell of gospel ministry (v 15-16)?

8. How do Paul's motives for ministry differ from the other preachers (v 17)?

⮕ apply

9. The Corinthians rejected Paul's authority and leadership because they thought him weak and unimpressive. What poor reasons might we use for not sitting humbly under those who teach us God's word?

⬆ pray

Give thanks that you, both as an individual and as part of a church, have received the grace, peace and mercy of God.

Pray for those who you know are going through difficult times. Pray that you would be part of the way the Lord comforts them, and that God would be helping them to grow in their ability to help others.

Praise God for your church leaders, and ask him to help them become more trustworthy and reliable in their work.

2

2 Corinthians 3 – 4
THE GOSPEL THAT CHANGES US

The story so far

Paul has been pleading with the Corinthian church to trust him, to stick with him, and to stick with the gospel. Suffering is an integral aspect of life and gospel ministry.

⊕ talkabout

1. What did you think of the gospel message when you first heard it?

• What has been your experience of sharing the gospel personally with others? How did they respond to you and the message?

⊥ investigate

▶ **Read 2 Corinthians 3:1-18**

There are different ways that someone can prove their credentials as a trustworthy teacher. In the ancient world, travelling philosophers used to carry letters of commendation from notable people.

2. What does Paul say his letters of recommendation are in verses 1-3?

    • How is this more powerful than any other letter written by other people?

3. What differences does Paul highlight between the ministries of the old and new covenant?

4. Why are people so hardened to the gospel (see also 4:4)?

    • How do people really change, and what results from it?

⊖ apply

5. What qualities should we look for in Bible teachers and Christian leaders if we are to trust them?

⊡ getting personal

Have you received the gospel of grace through Christ, or have you confused it, in part or in whole, with a rules-based misunderstanding of the Old Testament? How can you tell?

What do you think it means in practice to "contemplate the Lord's glory" (3:18)? How could you do this more?

⊡ explore more

❯ Read Exodus 34:29-34

optional

Why did Moses have to wear a veil over his face?

What does this show about God?

What does it show, ultimately, about the incompleteness of the Old Testament message?

⊡ investigate

❯ Read 2 Corinthians 4:1-18

6. How does the fact that people are blind to the truth affect Paul's attitude towards sharing the gospel message with others (3:12; 4:1, 16)?

- What is he prepared to endure in his gospel-sharing ministry and why (v 9-18)?

7. What does it take for someone to become a Christian (4:6)?

8. How does Paul think about the content of the gospel message?

- How might he be tempted to change it and why (v 2)?

➡ apply

9. What can we expect God to do in us and through us with the gospel?

• How should that be reflected in the way in which we live together as God's people?

10. How should this truth affect our attitude towards outreach and evangelism?

⊡ **getting personal**

Do you really expect God to change people you know and love through the gospel? Examine your own heart, and then lift them in prayer to God.

When are you tempted to change the gospel?

What do you need to remind yourself about when that happens?

⬆ **pray**

Spend some time beholding the glory of the Lord. Praise him for his greatness, goodness and love towards you in Christ.

Pray for family, friends and neighbours—that God would lift the veil from their eyes and reveal himself to them.

Pray that you would be bold in telling others the gospel, and be prepared to be weak and depend on God.

3 2 Corinthians 5
SEEING THE GOSPEL

The story so far

Paul is trying to win the Corinthians back to the cause of the gospel. He has shown how it is God's powerful way to save people. Now he goes on to spell out the content and challenge of the gospel message.

⊕ talkabout

1. What do you think heaven or the afterlife might be like? What views have you heard expressed about it?

• Are you looking forward to the future? Why/why not?

⊕ investigate

Paul describes our human bodies now as a "tent"—a temporary structure to house us—before we move into our eternal, permanent building in heaven (v 1). So how should we live now with this knowledge?

▶ **Read 2 Corinthians 5:1-10**

2. What differences are there between our life now "in tents", and our future life in God's eternal house (v 1)?

• Why do you think this life is characterised by "groaning" (v 2, 4)?

3. What will happen to followers of Christ when they die?

• How can we be confident about this (v 5)?

4. How should we respond to the knowledge that we will appear before the judgment seat of Christ (v 10)?

⊖ apply

5. "We live by faith, not by sight" (v 7). What might this mean in practical terms day by day?

⊡ getting personal

Would someone who observes your daily life conclude that you were living for the future?

Why is hope for the future such a powerful motivator?

Does it work like that for you?

⊕ investigate

❯ **Read 2 Corinthians 5:11-21**

6. Paul says that we should be committed to persuading others (v 11). What motivates him to do this (v 11, 14)?

7. What reasons does Paul give for why we should no longer regard people from a worldly point of view?

8. What privilege do we enjoy as those who are part of God's plan to reconcile the world to himself in Christ?

• How would you explain the gospel to someone using verse 21?

⮕ apply

9. What practical things will being an ambassador mean for you?

• What does it look like to "implore people" to be reconciled to God (v 20)?

10. How difficult do you find it to love others as Christ loves us?

⊡ getting personal

To what extent are you a people pleaser? How do you need to let the gospel reshape that?

Who do you need to start (or re-start) loving with Christ's love as you pursue their reconciliation with God?

⊡ explore more

optional

It might appear from verses 14-15 and 19 that everyone will be saved. Is that correct?

⊡ pray

Thank God that you can be confident of your future in Christ. Ask him to help you live by faith and not by sight. Ask God to give you his love for people who are lost. And thank God for the privilege of being an ambassador for him, and ask for opportunities to share the gospel message with others this week.

4 2 Corinthians 6 – 7
BE HAPPY

The story so far

Paul is pleading with the Corinthians to stick to the Gospel—God's powerful way to save people. He shows that believers have the enormous privilege of being made new, and having a role to play in bringing others to Christ.

⊕ talkabout

1. Who do you know who has given up significant things for the sake of the gospel? How has life worked out for them?

⊕ investigate

> **Read 2 Corinthians 6:1-13**

2. What does it mean that people can "receive God's grace in vain" (v 1)?

• What will prevent this from happening (v 2)?

3. Paul describes his experience as an ambassador of Christ in verses 3-10. How is each element of this list difficult to live out?

• How would you summarise the qualities that Paul has shown?

4. What does God promise us as those who are in Christ? What can we expect life to be like?

⊖ apply

5. How did you feel when you read Paul's description of his life? Did you find it attractive, astonishing, scary... or something else?

• How do you feel about the challenge to live life following Jesus in the same way that Paul followed him?

• Which aspect of Paul's description would you find most challenging personally and why?

⊡ **explore more**

optional

❯ **Read 2 Corinthians 6:14-18**

Why do you think Paul make this statement at this point in the chapter?

⊕ **investigate**

Paul has already shown us how we must pursue gospel integrity. He now moves on to speaking directly to the Corinthians about their relationship problems. In doing so he shows how we should all try to relate to one another as we seek to serve the Lord together.

❯ **Read 2 Corinthians 7:1-10**

6. What do you think it means to "make room for" someone in your heart (v 2)? Why had Paul been pushed out of their hearts?

> DICTIONARY
>
> **Repentance (v 9):** turning away from sin and towards God; living for him instead of ourselves.

7. How is it possible for a damaged relationship to be restored (v 4, 8, 9-10)?

8. What is the difference between godly sorrow and worldly sorrow (v 10)? Where does each lead?

• What happens when repentance is real (v 10-11)?

⤷ apply

9. Why do we struggle to say hard things to people, even to people we love? Why should we still do it?

10. Why do we settle for shallow apologies rather than the tears and joys of godly sorrow that brings repentance?

⊕ **pray**

Ask God to make you realistic about what it truly means to be a follower of Jesus and a bearer of the good news of Christ to others. Ask for the strength and faith to endure what God sends your way.

Pray for those you know who are struggling with opposition as they share the gospel.

Ask for God's help as you work to be reconciled to others that you have become estranged from. Pray that you would both embrace godly sorrow and repentance, and that you would experience the joy of reconciliation.

5 2 Corinthians 8 – 9
GIVE LIKE A MACEDONIAN

The story so far

Paul has laid out the nature, challenge and joys of living to serve God. He rejoices that his relationship with the Corinthians has been restored, and that they are partners together in the ministry of the gospel.

⊕ talkabout

1. A homeless person is sitting by the doorway of the supermarket as you walk in. His sign says, "Cold, hungry and poor". What feelings and conflicting emotions does this sight raise in you? What would you do?

⊕ investigate

▶ **Read 2 Corinthians 8:1-15**

2. What does sacrificial giving look like (v 1-4)?

DICTIONARY

Titus (v 6): at this point, Titus was a member of Paul's mission team.

3. According to Paul, what is the ultimate reason for giving sacrificially (v 9)?

4. Who and what should we give to?

⊟ apply

5. How does the example of the Macedonians inspire or worry you?

• What can stop us giving more generously?

⊡ getting personal

Think and pray about your giving. Ask the Lord to make you more generous as you consider Christ's gracious love and provision for you.

⊡ explore more

❯ **Read 2 Corinthians 8:13-24**

Paul gives a second example of gospel-hearted service.

What are the marks of trustworthy Christian service that Titus and others show?

What practical measures does Paul take to ensure that the money is correctly and responsibly handled?

⊡ investigate

❯ **Read 2 Corinthians 9:6-15**

6. What principles of giving does Paul lay out in verses 6-7?

> **DICTIONARY**
>
> **Sows (v 6):** plants seed.
> **Reap (v 6):** harvest.
> **Under compulsion (v 7):** feeling you have to.
> **Abound (v 8):** overflow; thrive.

7. What will be the end result of such giving (v 11, 12, 14, 15)?

8. Giving, according to Paul, is both good for us and promotes God's glory. How do these two work together?

➡ apply

9. How can we be a bit more "reckless" in our own giving? Give some practical examples.

10. How can we encourage each other to be more generous with what God has given to us, and encourage a spirit of generosity in our churches?

⊡ getting personal

When did you last review your personal giving?
Plan a time when you can contemplate the love, grace and generosity of the Lord Jesus to you, and then rethink your giving.

↑ pray

Ask God to raise up gospel workers of integrity, passion and determination in your church, who you will then generously send into the world. Pray that you would be one of them!

Give thanks for the goodness, grace and generosity of the Lord Jesus, who made himself poor so that you can be rich.

Ask the Lord to give you and your church a spirit of generosity, so that gospel workers will be supported and equipped to spread the good news, and the poor and needy helped.

6
2 Corinthians 10 – 11
THE BOASTING APOSTLE

The story so far

Paul is pleading with the Corinthians to follow him in living lives of genuine discipleship that follow the gospel in every area of life. But the problem of false teachers in their congregation still remains.

⊕ talkabout

1. How do people react when they are verbally attacked or criticised?

   • How do *you* react?

⊕ investigate

Paul's ministry and status as an apostle is being rejected by some of the Corinthians because they are more impressed with other teachers—"super apostles". In these chapters, Paul responds to the criticisms they make.

▶ **Skim-read 2 Corinthians 10; then read 2 Corinthians 11:1-15**

> **DICTIONARY**
>
> **Pretension (10:5):** proud claim.
> **Classify (10:12):** identify; group with.
> **Commend (10:12):** promote.
> **Sphere (10:13):** area.
> **Snake (11:3):** the devil (see Genesis 3:1-5; Revelation 12:9).
> **Sincere (11:3):** real, rather than faked.
> **Masquerading (11:13):** pretending to be; acting as.

2. By implication, what criticisms were being made about Paul in 11:6, 7, 8 (see also 10:1, 7)?

3. What does he say the "super-apostles" really are? What is their motivation and intention (11:13-14)?

- What will become of them in the end (v 15)?

4. How do we spot a false teacher, according to Paul?

⤴ apply

5. False teachers are still prevalent in our world. How can we spot them, and how can we resist their pull?

Have you ever been attracted to the message of a false teacher? What is it about their teaching that played to your pride, and took you away from the gospel? Where do you think you may still be vulnerable to listening to their teaching?

⊍ investigate

▶ **Read 2 Corinthians 11:16-33**

6. What has the life of Paul the apostle been like? Why does he list the physical dangers he has been in?

> **DICTIONARY**
>
> **Puts on airs (v 20):** pretends to be better than they are.
> **Abraham (v 22):** the ancestor of Israel.
> **Gentiles (v 26):** here, Paul is referring to non-Christian non-Jews.

7. What are the greater burdens he bears (v 28-29)?

• Why are these more difficult than the physical danger he has been in?

8. What would Paul much rather boast about and why (v 30)?

• What is the big principle here that he wants them (and us) to understand?

➡ apply

9. What do you think success is as a Christian? How will you need to think differently about that now?

▣ getting personal

What are you prone to boasting about as a Christian?

How will you need to adjust that in light of what you have just read?

10. What is going to be different this week as a result of what you have seen in this passage?

⬆ pray

Give thanks to God that he can use your weakness for his glory. Pray that you would be alert and aware of false teachers who aim to compromise the flock of God. And ask the Lord to give you the resilience and commitment to the gospel message that you see in Paul's life.

7 2 Corinthians 12 – 13
VISIONS AND VALUES

The story so far

Paul wants the Corinthians to see that the gospel must be applied in all of life. He is finishing his letter with an appeal to them to turn from their self-destructive ways, reject false teachers, and stick with the one true gospel.

⊕ talkabout

1. What has been your experience of good Christian leaders? What is it about them that you appreciated?

• What has been your experience of poor Christian leaders? Where did they go wrong, do you think?

⊕ investigate

▶ Read 2 Corinthians 12:1-10

2. Why does Paul start to "boast" about his spiritual experience in verses 1-4?

• What effect might this experience have had upon him (v 7)?

3. Why did God give Paul a "thorn in the flesh"?

• Why did God not take it away from him when Paul asked?

4. How does Paul summarise his views on strength, weakness and his suffering in the service of the gospel?

⤷ apply

5. What do Paul's experiences teach us about the highs and lows of our lives as Christians?

- Why is it so hard to embrace—let alone boast about—our weakness? What will bring us to the point that Paul reaches in verse 10?

⊡ getting personal

Do you need to repent of being "an idiot"—of looking at our world as if Christ had not died in our place, of being sucked in by people who are impressive but not godly? Do you need to ask God for the wisdom and strength in weakness to live a life which is shaped in every part by the cross of Christ.

⊥ investigate

▶ **Read 2 Corinthians 13:1-14**

6. Paul is preparing to visit the Corinthians again. What warnings does he give the church (v 1-3)?

> **DICTIONARY**
>
> **Testimony (v 1):** evidence.

- What will happen if they ignore the warnings and continue in their false ways?

7. What does Paul say they must do before he arrives (v 5)?

• What is his ultimate aim and motivation for saying this (v 7-10)?

8. How do Paul's final greetings and prayer (v 11-14) sum up what he wants to happen in the Corinthian church?

⮊ apply

9. All of us are more than capable of being selfish in relationships. What can motivate us to stick with difficult people as Paul did?

• If love builds, what is our primary responsibility to one another? How do you think we might do this?

10. For Paul, loving the Corinthians meant challenging them to be godly. How does this fit with your understanding of love?

- How does Paul's love for the Corinthians express itself in his prayers for them? What is the most loving thing we can pray for other people?

⊡ getting personal

Love can never be content to let relationships with brothers and sisters die. Is there a relationship we need to ask God for the grace to lovingly pursue and restore right now?

⊡ explore more

optional

▶ **Look back over the whole letter to remind yourself of its themes and teaching**

Take a moment to write down three key things that you have learned from 2 Corinthians about God, the gospel and the Christian life.

Now write down three things that God has challenged you to think and do differently in the power which he supplies in Christ through the Spirit.

⬆ pray

Use the words of 13:14 to pray for others in your group, in your church, and Christians the world over—especially those who are facing trials.

Pray that you would know the grace of Christ towards you—that he loves, forgives and accepts you through his finished work on the cross.

Pray that you would be convinced of the love of God for you. Even when you are facing trials from without, or perhaps have a "thorn in the flesh" within—pray that you would believe that these are given to you by God to help you walk humbly with him.

Pray that you would experience the fellowship of the Holy Spirit as you meet together, love one another, pray for one another, and worship Christ together.

The gospel in all of life
LEADER'S GUIDE

Leader's Guide

INTRODUCTION

Leading a Bible study can be a bit like herding cats—everyone has a different idea of what the passage could be about, and a different line of enquiry that they want to pursue. But a good group leader is more than someone who just referees this kind of discussion. You will want to:

- correctly understand and handle the Bible passage. But also...

- encourage and train the people in your group to do this for themselves. Don't fall into the trap of spoon-feeding people by simply passing on the information in the Leader's Guide. Then...

- make sure that no Bible study is finished without everyone knowing how the passage is relevant for them. What changes do you all need to make in the light of the things you have been learning? And finally...

- encourage the group to turn all that has been learned and discussed into prayer.

Your Bible-study group is unique, and you are likely to know better than anyone the capabilities, backgrounds and circumstances of the people you are leading. That's why we've designed these guides with a number of optional features. If they're a quiet bunch, you might want to spend longer on *talkabout*. If your time is limited, you can choose to skip *explore more*, or get people to look at these questions at home. Can't get enough of Bible study? Well, some studies have optional extra homework projects. As leader, you can adapt and select the material to the needs of your particular group.

So what's in the Leader's Guide? The main thing that this Leader's Guide will help you to do is to understand the major teaching points in the passage you are studying, and how to apply them. As well as guidance for the questions, the Leader's Guide for each session contains the following important sections:

THE BIG IDEA

One or two key sentences will give you the main point of the session. This is what you should be aiming to have fixed in people's minds as they leave the Bible study. And it's the point you need to head back toward when the discussion goes off at a tangent.

SUMMARY

An overview of the passage, including plenty of useful historical background information.

OPTIONAL EXTRA

Usually this is an introductory activity that ties in with the main theme of the Bible study, and is designed to "break the ice" at the beginning of a session. Or it may be a "homework project" that people can tackle during the week.

So let's take a look at the various different features of a Good Book Guide:

⊕ talkabout

Each session kicks off with a discussion question, based on the group's opinions or experiences. It's designed to get people talking and thinking in a general way about the main subject of the Bible study.

⊥ investigate

The first thing you and your group need to know is what the Bible passage is about, which is the purpose of these questions. But watch out—people may come up with answers based on their experiences or teaching they have heard in the past, without referring to the passage at all. It's amazing how often we can get through a Bible study without actually looking at the Bible! If you're stuck for an answer, the Leader's Guide contains guidance for questions. These are the answers to direct your group to. This information isn't meant to be read out to people—ideally, you want them to discover these answers from the Bible for themselves. Sometimes there are optional follow-up questions (see ⊗ in guidance for questions) to help you help your group get to the answer.

⊡ explore more

These questions generally point people to other relevant parts of the Bible. They are useful for helping your group to see how the passage fits into the "big picture" of the whole Bible. These sections are OPTIONAL—only use them if you have time. Remember that it's better to finish in good time having really grasped one big thing from the passage, than to try and cram everything in.

→ apply

We want to encourage you to spend more time working at application—too often, it is simply tacked on at the end. In the Good Book Guides, apply sections are mixed in with the investigate sections of the study. We hope that people will realise that application is not just an optional extra, but rather, the whole purpose of studying the

Bible. We do Bible study so that our lives can be changed by what we hear from God's word. If you skip the application, the Bible study hasn't achieved its purpose.

These questions draw out practical lessons that we can all learn from the Bible passage. You can review what has been learned so far, and think about practical differences that this should make in our churches and our lives. The group gets the opportunity to talk about what they personally have learned.

⊡ getting personal

These can be done at home, but it is well worth allowing a few moments of quiet reflection during the study for each person to think and pray about specific changes they need to make in their own lives. Why not have a time for reporting back at the beginning of the following session, so that everyone can be encouraged and challenged by one another to make application a priority?

⊕ pray

In Acts 4:25-30 the first Christians quoted Psalm 2 as they prayed in response to the persecution of the apostles by the Jewish religious leaders. Today however, it's not as common for Christians to base prayers on the truths of God's word as it once was. As a result, our prayers tend to be weak, superficial and self-centred rather than bold, visionary and God-centred.

The prayer section is based on what has been learned from the Bible passage. How different our prayer times would be if we were genuinely responding to what God has said to us through his word.

1 2 Corinthians 1 – 2
BEGINNING WITH GOD

THE BIG IDEA
The gospel comes with suffering and confusion, but God meets us and comforts us in our struggles. Suffering is part of the way that God helps us to grow more like Christ.

SUMMARY
Paul is writing to a church on the edge of disaster. When Paul showed up in Corinth for the first time, he found a city with a Roman face, a Greek heart, a large Jewish minority and a deeply ingrained universal desire to impress. It's hardly a shock then that when Paul preached the gospel and a church was born, life got pretty complicated. What else would you expect from a bunch of people who are mostly Greek, following a suffering and dying Jewish Messiah, in the middle of a Roman city which prides itself on always coming out on top. Welcome to the mess that is Corinth.

Church is always messy, but it's also true that some places are more messy than others. Corinth was one of those places. And Paul's relationship with the messy church he had planted in this complex city was—yes, you guessed it—messy.

After his initial stay in Corinth, when the church was planted (Acts 18:1-18), Paul heard that things had very quickly gone downhill. So about a year later, he wrote them a quick letter (now lost) explaining to them that sexual immorality in the church is not acceptable (he refers to that letter in 1 Corinthians 5:9).

That initial letter didn't do the trick, so about a year later (probably AD 53), he wrote the long letter that we know as 1 Corinthians, which covers a huge number of practical and theological issues.

You would hope that this might have fixed things in Corinth. But six months after that, Paul's apprentice, Timothy, passed through the port city and found that the church was in a complete mess. In fact, it was in such a mess that Paul dropped everything and made what he refers to in 2 Corinthians 2:1 as "the painful visit". Things did not go well, and it seems that Paul left Corinth unsure of whether the church would ever get back on track. His relationship with them was close to breaking point, and their grip on the gospel was weakening.

So he sent Titus with the letter he describes in 2:9. This letter seems to have had some positive effect, and so several months after that, sometime in late AD 54/55, two years after the church plant began and about a year after writing 1 Corinthians, Paul wrote 2 Corinthians (which confusingly was actually at least the fourth letter he'd written to them), which Titus again delivered.

It's important for us to appreciate this difficult history as we start to read 2 Corinthians because it goes some way to explaining why Paul both loved the Corinthians, and was driven nuts by them in equal measure. He has more recorded interaction with them than with any other church he planted. Their issues take up more of the New Testament than those of any other church. And at this point in their relationship, it was still not entirely clear whether the church would flourish and grow or crash and burn—which explains why this is the most passionate, honest, vulnerable, heartfelt letter in the Bible. The battle for hearts and minds was still on in Corinth. In particular, the leaders that Paul left behind continued to waver. So Paul wrote again in an attempt to persuade them to stick with him and with the gospel.

In the opening chapters of 2 Corinthians, Paul opens up the themes of suffering— both theirs and more particularly his own suffering for the sake of the gospel. He encourages them to see it, not as a negative sign that they have got things wrong, but that suffering is an inevitable part of gospel ministry—and a sign that he is faithfully engaged in God's work.

Note: 2 Corinthians is a long and complex letter with many difficult and nuanced passages. The aim of a study of this duration is to give an overall feel for the big issues and themes of this letter. This will inevitably mean skating over some of the detail, so there may well be many questions that come up in the study that are not covered in this guide. Please refer to *2 Corinthians For You.*

OPTIONAL EXTRA

Play a game of snakes and ladders, or another game where there are highs and lows, successes and failures. This will introduce the idea of struggle and pain being an inevitable part of life.

Note: This book and study deals with some heavyweight themes that your group may really struggle with. Be sensitive as you lead—do not push people to share particular struggles if they do not want to.

GUIDANCE FOR QUESTIONS

1. Why do you think church can be such a messy and difficult environment for people? What common problems can destroy a church if they are left unaddressed? Churches can be messy because people are messy! We can expect too much of each other, and allow our passion for the gospel to lead to division. Overbearing leadership or sin which is allowed to flourish unchecked can also cause long-term problems. Don't let the group spend too long on this question, and don't allow people to criticise other churches without seeing any problems that might be alive in your own congregation.

2. What do the opening two verses suggest are some of the issues that need to be addressed in Corinth? Paul's apostleship has been questioned by the Corinthian church so he makes it clear that this is something that he received from God. He also underlines that this church is not *their* church, but belongs to God. He finishes the introduction by making it clear that he wants them to experience the grace and peace of God, together with him.

3. Grace and peace are the twin marks of the local church, according to Paul. How does the gospel produce these key features? We receive grace from God in the way he forgives us through Christ. We experience peace with God through Christ's death on the cross. Those who follow Christ should behave towards others with the same qualities that Christ has shown to us. We should be gracious and forgiving of others. We should be seeking peace and harmony in the local church, as this is what God wants for us. This love for one another is something that God pours into our hearts by the Holy Spirit. Christ-like leadership is so important in all of this. Those who are appointed as "under-shepherds of the flock" (1 Peter 5:2) should show the same grace and self-sacrificial attitude in their ministry as Jesus did.

4. Who comforts whom in these verses? And why do they need to be comforted? God comforts us in our afflictions so that we are able to comfort others who are going through times of trouble. Suffering that we experience in the context of Christian ministry and service is, in some way, actually sharing in the sufferings of Christ. Paul seems to suggest that suffering is intimately bound up with being a Christian in this life.

• **What aspects of God's character does Paul highlight here?** God is described as the father of compassion and the God of all comfort. Even in our darkest moments, we can know that God is able to meet us in our need. When we suffer, we can know that God is not being angry with us or vengeful towards us. He is the God of all mercy.

• **How should our view of God and suffering change in light of these truths?** Suffering is an inevitable part of life, but also an inevitable part of the Christian life—because what happened to our master is what will happen to us. We should count it a privilege to share in Christ's sufferings. Through our trials, and the experience of receiving comfort and encouragement from God, we are also being trained and equipped to encourage and help others. Suffering should draw Christians together in love and mutual support.

5. APPLY: What is the worst thing you have ever suffered? Did you experience the love and comfort of God as you were going through it? Be sensitive in how you deal with this! Some may be able to testify to God's goodness to them in difficult circumstances (bereavement, unemployment, being rejected by friends,

etc.); but it is possible that some felt abandoned by God. Try to draw out the lessons from any negatives—perhaps God's people were lax in offering help and hospitality, for example.

• **How are we able to show the love and comfort of God to others who are in distressing circumstances?** Encourage the group to think of practical ways that they can offer comfort—listening to, praying for, and speaking the words of the gospel, where appropriate, are good things to do. But so also is practical help with food, cleaning, child-care, etc.

EXPLORE MORE
Why does Paul write so much to them about how his travel plans had changed, do you think? Paul has been under the critical scrutiny of the Corinthians, who have labelled him as untrustworthy because his plans changed. Paul s showing why these changes were reasonable, and motivated by love and gospel concern for others.
What comes out of this section about how trustworthy and accountable Christian leaders should be? Christian leaders should be sincere (1:12-14); have a dependable flexibility (1:15-22); exhibit robust love (1:23 – 2:11); and demonstrate real care for individuals (2:12-13).

6. Who leads this procession and what is the aroma they spread? Jesus is the victor, and Paul, other Christian leaders, and all Christians are those who are swinging the incense burners that proclaim his victory. We make the "smell" of the gospel as we tell others that Jesus Christ has won the victory over sin, death and the Satan.

7. How do different groups respond to the smell of gospel ministry (v 15-16)? For those who are on the side of the victor, the aroma is a pleasing reminder that Jesus has won, and that therefore we have won as well. But for those who are against him, the smell of gospel ministry is a reminder that they will be put to death as enemies of the victorious Christ. No wonder therefore that true gospel ministry incites such love and such hatred.

8. How do Paul's motives for ministry differ from the other preachers (v 17)? Unpick what this verse says phrase by phrase. They do not "sell" the gospel like so many other travelling teachers did in the ancient world. They are sincere in what they do. Their commission comes from God, and their message is about Christ,

not themselves. They conduct their ministry knowing that they are serving God himself.

9. APPLY: What poor reasons might we use for not sitting humbly under those who teach us God's word? Like the Corinthians, we might feel that our leaders are not impressive enough to warrant our respect. Or we may disagree with their strategy or the way they conduct themselves in their public or private lives. We should learn to encourage and help our leaders as those who have been appointed by God, and who bear a heavy burden in caring for the flock, and who suffer for their pains in ministry.

2 2 Corinthians 2 – 4
THE GOSPEL THAT CHANGES US

THE BIG IDEA
We can be confident in the gospel, and therefore in our evangelism, because the gospel brings genuine change in people.

SUMMARY
In his letters, and perhaps here in 2 Corinthians above all others, Paul has a highly nuanced attitude to "self-commendation". As we have already seen, Paul has no problem in defending himself, backing himself and even boasting, when it is clear that his boasting flows from what God has done in us and for us through the Lord Jesus Christ. So boasting is fine when it is boasting about Christ. Self-defence

is fine when it is really standing for the gospel. For Paul, even self-commendation is OK, if it is based on the fact that God himself has commissioned us, as in 2:17. It's useful to know that in the first century, self-commendation was entirely appropriate when trying to sort out a relational issue. Which gives 3:1 the sense *Am I commending myself? You bet I am!*

Travelling philosophers would bring with them elaborate letters of commendation. Paul goes down a different route: in 3:2, he says that the Corinthians themselves are the only credentials that he needs. Paul knows that people matter to God, and so people matter to him. That's why he describes God as having inscribed this letter on his heart and those of his team. It's a graphic picture. And it's a striking reminder that authentic ministry is *about people*.

The lasting fruit of our lives will be people. People whom God has changed through the gospel spoken by us and our brothers and sisters. For Paul, the primary reason that the Corinthians should continue to listen to him was that God had spoken through him when he first proclaimed the gospel to them. He was a flawed messenger, but God brought them to life and formed a church through his preaching.

He then goes on to compare the Old and New Covenant. Paul isn't writing a theological treatise on the role of the law versus the role of the Spirit here—he is addressing the question of how we can have a realistic view of ourselves and yet get on with ministry without being crippled by doubt or guilt. And his answer? We can get on with it because God has given us a "New Covenant" ministry, which is centred on the fact that God speaks through the message of Jesus' death and resurrection to bring people to new life.

What Paul says here about our ministry is staggering. God reveals his glory in Christ through the gospel. When Christ is preached, God works by the Spirit to show people how stunningly gloriously beautiful Christ is. We should keep going because the ministry which God has given us reveals the glory of God in the face of Christ, and there is no greater beauty, no greater privilege, no greater experience for human beings than this.

OPTIONAL EXTRA

Get the group to write down an unusual fact about how they have changed. *I used to… but now I…* Pick the pieces of paper out one by one, and read them out. The group has to guess who in the group has written it. You could follow up with gentle questions like, *Why/how did this change happen? Was it difficult or easy?*

GUIDANCE FOR QUESTIONS

1. What did you think of the gospel message when you first heard it?
• **What has been your experience of sharing the gospel personally with others? How did they respond to you and the message?**

These questions are designed to bring out the variety of responses to the gospel. When some first hear it, they think it is stupid, outrageous or even evil. Others are drawn to it or intrigued by it. There will be similar stories of how others have responded as we have made attempts to share the good news with others.

2. What does Paul say his letters of recommendation are in verses 1-3?
His letters are the Corinthians themselves. He preached the gospel to them, it took root in their lives, and they became Christians by the power of the Spirit. It shows that his message is from God and that he has been appointed by God to preach the gospel. Paul also alludes to another proof—his ongoing love for the Corinthians, as evidenced by his perseverance with them. This is proven by his many visits and letters. Paul also shows his genuineness by his humility about his own abilities. It is God doing the work through him. He is not confident in himself, but in Christ.

• **How is this more powerful than any other letter written by other people?**
This is God's endorsement on his ministry. Other human opinions may count for something, but far less than God's endorsement. This endorsement is shown

through Paul's faithfulness to the message, his love for those he is serving and the reality of the faith of those who heard and received the message.

3. What differences does Paul highlight between the ministries of the old and new covenant? The Old Testament message is that through obedience to the law you can attain righteousness. It is mediated by a letter (the written law). But this is impossible. The sacrificial system was to show that only through God accepting a substitute could people be forgiven and be reconciled to God. The New Testament message is that through Christ, we can find forgiveness and new life. It is mediated by the Spirit. Paul draws many contrasts. The letter (of the law) kills; the Spirit brings life. The OT message was glorious; but the NT message is more glorious. The letter is a ministry of condemnation; the Spirit is a ministry that brings righteousness. The letter was temporary; the Spirit is permanent.

4. Why are people so hardened to the gospel (see also 4:4)? Paul is particularly talking here about the response of Jewish people who know and are committed to the Old Testament message—but it is true for all people. There is a veil over their hearts, and their minds are hardened. People are blind to the gospel.

• **How do people really change, and what results from it?** The veil of blindness is removed as people turn to the Lord Jesus Christ (v 16). As people respond to the gospel message that Jesus is Lord and turn to him in repentance and faith, they find freedom from enslavement to the law as a way of getting right with him. They can look God in the face, knowing that they are truly forgiven by Christ alone, by faith alone, by grace alone. And this

change continues as they continue to "gaze" at God.

5. APPLY: What qualities should we look for in Bible teachers and Christian leaders if we are to trust them? The qualities that we see in Paul. Are they hard working, are they faithful to the gospel of the New Testament? Do they preach law, or do they preach the free gift of God through Christ in a message mediated by the Spirit? Are they humble? Do they show loving commitment for those they teach? Do they persevere in reaching out to those they minister to, with concern for their spiritual welfare? Are those who are converted under their ministry healthy, freedom-loving disciples of Christ, or are they legalistic?

EXPLORE MORE
Read Exodus 34: 29-34
Why did Moses have to wear a veil over his face? Moses literally glowed because he had met God. The people were fearful, which showed that they were estranged from God. Moses covered up in order to protect them. It shows that the OT message did not lead to people being reconciled to God.
What does this show about God? God is awesome, and holy. We cannot approach him without our sins having been dealt with.
What does it show, ultimately, about the incompleteness of the Old Testament message? The sacrificial system points to Christ, but could never result in forgiveness. It pointed to the greater sacrifice that Christ made on the cross which fulfilled all the promises of the Old Testament.

6. How does the fact that people are blind to the truth affect Paul's attitude towards sharing the gospel message with others (3:12; 4:1, 16). He has hope that blind, resistant people can be changed by God, and so he preaches the gospel with boldness, and does not lose heart if they do not respond.

- **What is he prepared to endure in his gospel-sharing ministry and why (v 9-18)?** Paul is prepared to suffer an enormous amount, because sharing the good news about Christ is so important. Sharing the gospel is the way that people receive eternal life, and God is glorified in it and through it. He also has a deep love for everyone who is lost, and a love for God as he is obedient to his calling.

7. What does it take for someone to become a Christian (4:6)? God has to open their eyes in an act that is equivalent of creation. It is God's work, not ours. Our job is to proclaim the gospel fearlessly, faithfully and without adornment. Jesus Christ is Lord.

8. How does Paul think about the content of the gospel message (v 1-5)? He doesn't try to change it, but knows he has to be faithful to the message. He presents it simply, plainly and humbly. Jesus Christ is Lord.

- **How might he be tempted to change it and why (v 2)?** When people don't respond to Christ, we might be tempted to think that the message is wrong or defective, and so we try to fix it ourselves. We do this either by changing it, or by using manipulative tricks. We might change it to bring glory to ourselves, rather than God. Paul rejects these things because he knows that it is God who is doing the work of opening blind eyes. Only God's gospel is able to truly save people, so it is counterproductive to change it or rely on human techniques.

9. APPLY: What can we expect God to do in us and through us with the gospel? Even for people who we think are completely hardened to the gospel, God can change them as he changed Paul and us.

- **How should that be reflected in the way in which we live together as God's people?** We should be committed as a fellowship to the task of outreach and evangelism, being kind and open, even to those who oppose or mock us. It also means that we should be prayerful, looking to God who changes people, and not relying on techniques, programmes or our gifts.

10. APPLY: How should this truth affect our attitude towards outreach and evangelism? Evangelism is always hard. We will always meet opposition, misunderstanding and mockery. We can easily lose heart if we keep our eyes fixed on our own weakness, failure and the lack of response. But if we keep our eyes fixed on God and put our confidence in him, we will not lose heart, and may even become bolder in declaring Jesus as Lord to others. God is powerful to save. We are weak, but our weakness is part of God's strategy—he brings glory to himself as we share the gospel with others in our weakness.

3 2 Corinthians 5
SEEING THE GOSPEL

THE BIG IDEA

Belonging to Christ will always be deeply and profoundly counter-cultural. The gospel confronts us and re-orientates our lives so that we are now focused on the future not the present; we fear God not other people; we love others as we follow Christ; and we pursue gospel relationships relentlessly.

SUMMARY

In chapter 5 Paul shows how the gospel challenges us and confronts us to live in four ways that are different to how we naturally live as sinners in a fallen world.

1. We look to the future. Living to please someone else gets a bad press these days. In the 21st century, our wellbeing is routinely tied to pleasing ourselves. We are to focus on our own self-actualisation, and self-affirmation and a thousand other forms of self-focus. One of the many problems with this is that it is entirely focused on the present—the Corinthians (like most of us) would have loved it. But not Paul. He urges the Corinthians, and us, to go against our natural grain and look to the future. This is not our real home, we are looking to the future to come.

2. We fear God not people. Fearing people does so much damage to our lives. It stops our evangelism in its tracks, it hamstrings our ability to lead, it stops us saying the hard thing, and pushes us into living for the approval of others. But thank God that in Christ, we have no need to act like that, because Christ has died and risen, we are united to him, and so we fear God alone.

3. We love people like Christ loves us. In verse 14, Paul says that the love of Christ controls us. We no longer look at others in the way we used to—judging, discarding, liking or loathing depending on our view of them. We see people as Christ sees them. They are precious souls, and we must love them as Christ loves them, and be prepared to give ourselves for them in the same way that Christ gave himself for us.

4. We pursue gospel relationships. The chapter ends with the declaration that we are ambassadors for Christ in his work of reconciling people to God. This should be thought of less as an official role and title, and more as a way that our goal in life is to pursue relationships that bring the gospel message to people and in turn people to God. Because Jesus' work of reconciliation, his sin-bearing, righteousness-giving, relationship-restoring work on the cross and in his resurrection, we are people who relentlessly pursue gospel relationships. We are those who are prepared to face pain, and say hard things, and take the initiative over and over again, to pursue things until they are right, because this is the way of the gospel.

OPTIONAL EXTRA

Ask the group about hobbies or interests that they are passionate about. It might be photography, fishing, impressionist paintings, football or chess. Get a couple of them to "sell" their interest to the others. The aim of the exercise is to see how unembarrassed and passionate they are about their chosen subject—something we often find difficult when we are put in the position of talking to others about the gospel.

GUIDANCE FOR QUESTIONS

1. What do you think heaven or the afterlife might be like? What views have you heard expressed about it? Take a note of the views expressed. Some may be faulty biblically. Now is not the time to challenge them, but it would be worth following up later with someone who has a erroneous or incomplete view.

• **Are you looking forward to the future? Why/why not?** The aim of this introductory question is to get people thinking about the future. We tend to be centred in the now, and this will be challenged directly by the passage that we are reading.

2. What differences are there between our life now "in tents", and our future life in God's eternal house (v 1)? Our tent (body) will be destroyed; our home in heaven is permanent and eternal. We would prefer to be at home with the Lord but must stay in the tent of this earthly life.

• **Why do you think this life is characterised by "groaning" (v 2, 4)?** We live in a sinful world, and our life now is characterised by weakness and death. We long to be with Christ, but we are called to live now and share the gospel message of life with others. Paul describes his ministry as a kind of dying. But it is dying with a purpose. So the nature of Christian "groaning" has a hopeful quality to it.

3. What will happen to followers of Christ when they die? Paul likens it to changing a temporary tent to a permanent home with the Lord. He also likens it to being naked, and putting on a further layer of clothing.

• **How can we be confident about this (v 5) ?** God has given us his Spirit as a guarantee. The work of God's Spirit in our lives, to make us holy, to make us alive to God, to call God "father", to give us love for one another, to join us together in the church, are all signs that we have received the Spirit, and that we are therefore destined for eternal life.

4. How should we respond to the knowledge that we will appear before the judgment seat of Christ (v 10)? We should not fear. This is not the judgment of condemnation, because we know that we have been saved for all eternity by Christ— "we are confident" (v 8). But the implication is that there will be some kind of assessment, and reward, as we enter eternity. Rather than fear, this thought should encourage us to work hard please him (v 9).

5. APPLY: "We live by faith, not by sight" (v 7). What might this mean in practical terms day by day? Christians should be those who live for the future, and not for today. The future is, by definition, unseen. When we live for today, and not for the future, we will tend to live for what we see, and become engrossed in the physical world and our bodies. When we live by faith, we live believing in the promises of God that the future is the goal of our lives, not the present. This can have radical and profound implications. Eternity will be the place where all our desires will be met; so there is no reason to seek all the world's pleasures now. No need for a bucket list. We can happily deny ourselves for the sake of the gospel, knowing that our future will provide everything and more.

6. Paul says that we should be committed to persuading others (v 11). What motivates him to do this (v 11, 14)? The fear of the Lord (v 11). This is not a fear of punishment or rejection. This is the fear of knowing how great and good God is, and responding to him appropriately. "Christ's love compels us" (v 14). We have experienced the astonishing and grace-filled love of Jesus Christ. We know that Jesus' love extends even to his enemies (enemies like we once were)—and so we cannot hate or dismiss others. We must love them as Christ loves them. And the greatest way we can love them is to share the gospel with them that can reconcile them to God.

7. What reasons does Paul give for why we should no longer regard people from a worldly point of view? The subject here is those who are Christian believers. Christ died for all of us so that we should no longer live for ourselves, but for Christ who died for us and was raised again (v 15). How should we now think of other people, both Christian and non-Christian? We look at everyone through the lens of the gospel. People are no longer good or bad, nice or nasty, wealthy or poor, "useful" to us, or of no interest. How they relate to Christ is the most important thing. If they are in Christ, they are brothers and sisters, whatever their past. They are new creations (v 17). If they are not in Christ, then God has called us to work for their reconciliation to him, by living, sharing, preaching and teaching the gospel message.

8. What privilege do we enjoy as those who are part of God's plan to reconcile the world to himself in Christ? We are Christ's ambassadors, making the appeal to "be reconciled to God" through the death and resurrection of Jesus Christ. Our role is to implore people to be reconciled to God.

• **How would you explain the gospel to someone using verse 21?** This is about the cross, and the substitution that Jesus

made for us there. He was made sin for us, when he had no sin himself, so that, in him, we become righteous (= right with God). If you know "The Book" illustration, this would be a good explanation to do with your group now. You can find a version of it for download in the extras here: www.thegoodbook.co.uk/2-corinthians-the-gospel-in-all-of-life

9. APPLY: What practical things will being an ambassador mean for you? It means knowing what our mission, identity and purpose is in the world. It means being committed to Christ's kingdom, not the passing and failing kingdom of this world. It means realising that we have an honour and privilege that we can be proud of in the right way, because it comes to us by grace, not merit. It means bearing our office with dignity, seriousness, love and concern to bring glory and honour to Christ. It means never being off-duty, and always remembering that to other people, we represent our King: they will judge the Kingdom of God by how we behave.

• **What does it look like to "implore people" to be reconciled to God (v 20)?** The word "implore" indicates that this is not a "take it or leave it" message. It is something that is life and death; of eternal importance. We should use our every effort to engage and intrigue people, so that they ponder, question and receive the gospel message. But we do this in a loving way, and with dignity and respect as Christ's ambassadors: not as shrill unthinking proclaimers.

10. APPLY: How difficult do you find it to love others as Christ loves us? What will help you love them more? It is hard to love the unlovely, or those who have wronged or hurt us. But if we look at them through the lens of the Gospel, everything changes. We were unlovely, but Christ loved us. We were lost, but Jesus found us. We were hostile and difficult, but God was patient with us, and reconciled us to himself. With the gospel of Christ in the front of our minds as we relate to others, we will have both the motivation and the message that we need to share.

EXPLORE MORE

It might appear from verses 14-15 and 19 that everyone will be saved. Is that correct? When he says "Christ died for all"—does he mean everyone without exception? Was Paul a universalist? Or given the fact that in verse 15, he is clearly talking about believers, did Christ die for everyone but was only raised for believers? These are tricky questions that have divided people over the years. But the most natural way to read these verses is as referring to the same group of people all the way through—namely, Christian believers, for whom Christ died and rose again. His point then is that, having been united with Christ by faith in his death and resurrection, we have already died to ourselves, and the only real option for us is to live for Christ, which, as Paul goes on to explain, means loving other people. If we take this on board, we will refuse to look at anyone according to the flesh (v 16). Paul adds that we (meaning himself in particular) got it so spectacularly wrong about Jesus, that it has cured us of making damning judgments about anyone else.

4 2 Corinthians 6 – 7
BE HAPPY

THE BIG IDEA

Gospel ministry is a huge privilege, but it is also very costly. Radical discipleship involves obedience to Christ in response to his grace, and a commitment to making the gospel known—it is the only way to real joy.

SUMMARY

2 Corinthians chapters 1 – 6 are just about the most raw, full-on, up-close-and-personal, deeply-intense chapters of the New Testament. Paul has been fighting desperately to win the hearts and minds of the church family in Corinth, and we have got the strong sense that for most of the book so far, he hasn't had any real confidence that it was going to come off.

The future of the church he had planted seems to be up in the air. He is laying everything on the line to help them stay on track, and then suddenly, just like that, the mood changes, and the apostle is apparently dancing for joy! What's going on?

The explanation is quite straightforward. Life is complex. Even when we are facing big issues, it's never the whole story. Sometimes we are facing a huge problem, but once we've dealt with that, the underlying situation is really quite encouraging. And that's exactly what's happening here. For the first 6 chapters, Paul is speaking to those who are wavering—the people who have been influenced by their city and their favourite philosophers, and aren't too sure about Paul—but now, we get the rest of the picture. Chapter 6 outlines what committed gospel ministry may look like. He has suffered enormously for the gospel, and has been totally committed to integrity, purity, holiness and hard work. And yet Paul is happy. And as he rejoices, the apostle maps out what it takes for all of us to be joyful servants of the Lord Jesus.

Paul deals with, responds to and encourages the errant Corinthians, but he doesn't really tell us much about them. He does show us how he operates, and provides us with a template for a lifetime of joyful gospel ministry. There is plenty of suffering and opposition. But for Paul, there is always real joy in ministry even as we suffer, and he gives us 4 steps to joy:

1. Pursue integrity.
2. Invest in people.
3. Say what needs to be said.
4. Seek joy through repentance.

These are the clear notes he keeps striking in these two chapters.

OPTIONAL EXTRA

Play a couple of songs with "Happiness" in the title. e.g. "Happy" by Pharrell Williams; "Happiness" by Ken Dodd, "Don't Worry, Be Happy" by Bobby McFerrin. Ask the group to work out what the recipe is for happiness in each of these songs.

GUIDANCE FOR QUESTIONS

1. Who do you know who has given up significant things for the sake of the gospel? How has life worked out for them? Some of the group will know a missionary or other Christian who has moved away from a significant career or life of ease to do something hard, dangerous or difficult for the Lord. Often their parents and friends do not understand, and they can

labour for years without seeing much fruit. Prepare a story yourself in case no one has any personal knowledge of someone like this. The aim is to show that what Paul writes about in these chapters then is also real now.

2. What does it mean that people can "receive God's grace in vain" (v 1)? People can have an experience of the gospel, be excited by it, love the fellowship of the church and be moved by it emotionally, but it does not change them deep inside. They may appear to be converted, but the grace of God has had no deep effect on them. To all intents and purposes, they will appear to have become Christians, but will not stick at it, like the seed sown in the rocky soil in Jesus' famous parable (see Mark 4: 1-20, especially verses 5-6, 16-17).

• **What will prevent this from happening (v 2)?** Paul quotes Isaiah, but applies it to the present moment. His point is that God speaks to us in the here and now, not just in history. The way of discipleship is the way of listening to God speak in the here and now, every day and responding on the spot. The alternative is to slip into a dangerously Corinthian mentality, where we say (usually silently), I know you are speaking to me Lord—I have taken a note of it and will respond in due course! But when God addresses us, it has to take priority over everything.

3. Paul describes his experience as an ambassador of Christ in verses 3-10. How is each element of this list difficult to live out? You could spend a lot of time working through this list, highlighting the nuance of every term that Paul uses. Each trial required enormous determination, humility, and commitment to Christ and his ways. Note that he is not just enduring outward physical threats, but inward battles against impure thoughts and temptations—to lie, to be impatient, to lack kindness and love towards those he is seeking to serve for Christ's sake. Perhaps most difficult of all is being misunderstood by those, like the Corinthians, who he is sharing his life with. He is straining every fibre to be sincere and genuine, but they think him a fake, and reject him.

- **How would you summarise the qualities that Paul has shown?** Faithfulness, authenticity, integrity. This is what God is calling us to. We might be tempted to think that this kind of life is totally beyond us, and yet it is not. Make sure the group understands that the details of Paul's discipleship are so dramatic because of the particular role he was called to, and the culture he lived in. But each element of his life is something we can live out now.

4. What does God promise us as those who are in Christ? What can we expect life to be like? You could summarise by asking four questions which flow out of the four movements of the list: 1. Are you ready for the rest of your life to be hard? 2. Are you committed to using only gospel-shaped means and methods in ministry? 3. Are you prepared for the fact that you will be praised and damned in equal measure? 4. Are you convinced that you can only find security and satisfaction in Christ?

5. APPLY: How did you feel when you read Paul's description of his life? Did you find it attractive, astonishing, scary … or something else? This question is designed for you to get a feel for where individuals in the group are in their discipleship. Are they trying to have the best of both worlds, which means compromising on the gospel? Or are they sincerely trying their best, in difficult circumstances?

- **How do you feel about the challenge to live life following Jesus in the same way that Paul followed him?**
- **Which aspect of Paul's description would you find most challenging personally?** Allow the group to talk about where the challenge of discipleship impacts them most powerfully from these two questions. Allow God's word to do its work of challenging the group.

EXPLORE MORE
Why does Paul make this statement at this point in the chapter? These verses are often used to argue in detail about marrying or going into business with a non-believer. But in this context it is the bigger picture Paul is looking at—the Corinthians , and perhaps us too, want to have their cake and eat it. They want the comfort, forgiveness and community of belonging to Christ, but also their comfortable life of privilege. Paul tells them that they cannot enjoy both together and must choose.

6. What do you think it means to "make room for" someone in your heart (v 2)? Why had Paul been pushed out of their hearts? They have had a difficult relationship, where some have criticised Paul, or doubted his motives, or thought he was not impressive enough. And because Paul was persistent in seeking to maintain the relationship, they had perhaps grown tired, bored or resistant to him. Paul is pleading for them to behave Christianly in their relationship with him. They must love him, and forgive whatever offence (real or imagined) they feel towards him.

7. How is it possible for a damaged relationship to be restored? There needs to be truth telling and honesty (v 4). There needs to be an open expression of the differences and disagreements, even if those things hurt. Paul put these things in his difficult letter (v 8), that caused them sorrow. But he spoke the truth in love in order to lead them to repentance (v 9-10). And finally there needs to be genuine repentance—genuine sorrow at wrongdoing that leads to a change of mind and a change of heart and behaviour.

8. What is the difference between godly sorrow and worldly sorrow (v 10)? Where does each lead? Worldly sorrow is just being sorry that something happened, or about what has resulted. It does not lead to change, and therefore it leads to death. Godly sorrow sees that our sin is at the heart of what has gone wrong. It leads to genuine repentance and change.

• **What happens when repentance is real (v 10-11)?** People change. Relationships are restored. People are encouraged. The gospel work goes forward. Point out to the group that there is a note of joy in this chapter. Genuine repentance leads not to grudging forgiveness and ongoing distrust. It leads to genuine fellowship, joy and

renewed commitment.

9. APPLY: Why do we struggle to say hard things to people, even to people we love? Why should we still do it? Many reasons. Fear of what will result. We can assume that they will not respond and it will be difficult or embarrassing. We can be fearful that we will be rejected. We can worry that there will be angry outbursts. We can be too proud to take the first step. Perhaps we have just given up on them. We must do it, because it is the only way that gospel reconciliation can take place.

10. APPLY: Why do we settle for shallow apologies rather than the tears and joys of godly sorrow that brings repentance? It is mainly pride, and a sense of comfort with where we are. We excuse ourselves, and do not recognise the depth of our own sinfulness and involvement in broken relationships. We can also be fearful that genuine repentance means stepping outside of our comfort zone with regard to our witness and lives.

5 2 Corinthians 8 – 9
GIVE LIKE A MACEDONIAN

THE BIG IDEA
Christians should be open-hearted, whole-hearted gospel-hearted followers of Christ. This includes how we think about and use the financial resources that God has given us.

SUMMARY
It's easy to forget that these letters aren't

just abstract theoretical treatises which lay the theological foundation for Christianity (which they do). They are also real letters, written for pressing and urgent reasons—in this case, to get the prosperous Corinthians to part with large amounts of their hard-earned cash so that their poor brothers back in Jerusalem could put some food on their table. Paul wrote to make sure that when Titus and his friends showed up, they would be prepared, and there would be a large pile of drachma waiting for them.

However, in tackling this slightly embarrassing issue, Paul gives us a stunning model of applying the gospel to a real-world, real-time situation. And as he does this, it becomes apparent that, while money is the presenting issue, for Paul these chapters are basically a call to be open-hearted, whole-hearted, gospel-hearted followers of Jesus. This will show in the way they handle their money.

Paul uses the gospel generosity of the Macedonians as an example (8:1-7). Their giving was sacrificial, enthusiastic and spiritual—they were genuinely joyful in their giving.

Ultimately, Jesus is our model for sacrificial giving (8:9-15). In one brief sentence (8:9), Paul declares the pre-existence of the Son and the grace which God has shown to us in the incarnation and Jesus' death in our place. In response, he urges the Corinthians—and us—to be selfless and to add to the collection.

OPTIONAL EXTRA

Give everyone the same number of tokens or equal amounts of monopoly money. Put four pots on the table marked as:
1. Poverty relief. 2. Medical research.
3. Gospel work overseas. 4. Guide Dogs for the Blind. Get people to split their money and put it in the pots they would most want to give to. Afterwards, discuss the motives for their choices. Why did they choose some, not others?

GUIDANCE FOR QUESTIONS

1. A homeless person is sitting by the doorway of the supermarket as you

walk in. His sign says "Cold, hungry and poor". What feelings and conflicting emotions does this sight raise in you? What would you do? Many people feel conflicted by this question. We are called to be generous and give to the poor. We are called to have compassion on the poor and needy. Yet we are worried that any money we give might go towards alcohol or drugs, or be perpetuating a social system that keeps people on the streets. Some may offer to buy food. Others give money and walk quickly away. Others will take the time to sit down and talk with them. Loneliness and lack of human connections is often a bigger problem than hunger. Few answers are wrong here, but this will set the context for our priorities in giving that we will discuss later in this study.

2. What does sacrificial giving look like? The Macedonians were themselves poor, and going through a time of extreme trial. But they gave generously, joyfully, out of their poverty. They thought giving was a privilege. Their understanding of the gospel and their gratitude to God led them to have an intimate connection with their brothers and sisters far away who were in need. They even pleaded with Paul to be able to give (v 4).

3. According to Paul, what is the ultimate reason for giving sacrificially? The grace of God shown to us in Christ (8:9). The pre-existent Son of God left glory to be born as a human, and to die in our place on the cross. He is our model for living. So Paul urges the Corinthians—and us—to be selfless and to add to the collection. In particular, they need to make sure they follow through on their pledges.

4. Who and what should we give to? This particular collection was for the relief of starving Christians in Jerusalem, where there was a famine. The general principle in the New Testament is that we should "do good to all people—especially those of the household of faith" (Galatians 6:10). God is pleased when we care for the poor and needy, but we do need to prioritise the work of the gospel. Many people will give to famine relief, Children in Need and disaster relief. Only Christians will give towards gospel work. In the same way that we should never neglect our human families as we seek to do good to those in need, we must also not neglect to supply the needs of our Christian family—especially those who are engaged in the work of gospel outreach.

5. APPLY: How does the example of the Macedonians inspire or worry you? Some people might find it difficult to understand how they could be so generous. This is possibly because we have failed to appreciate how generous God has been to us in Christ. Encourage the group to be inspired by their example, and seek the same motivation they had, rather than feel like failures, or that the Macedonians' level of commitment is unattainable.

• **What can stop us giving more generously?** Allow people to give their reasons, but then guide them back to a lack of appreciation for how generous God has been to us.

EXPLORE MORE
What are the marks of trustworthy Christian service that Titus and others show? They are committed, hard working, humble, gospel-focused and prepared to endure hardship—everything that Paul has been laying out as the marks of true discipleship in this letter.
What practical measures does Paul take to ensure that the money is correctly

and responsibly handled? He gives over the responsibility to someone else who is trusted. Why is he so passionate about this? Because he knows that fights and accusations about money will kill off gospel ministry more quickly than almost anything else. When it comes to money, we need to be beyond reproach, because only then will people be able to see that the gospel produces servant-heartedness.

6. What principles of giving does Paul lay out in verses 6-7? God loves generosity, but we there is also much we will gain ourselves as we give. Not giving is robbing yourself! We also need to have integrity in giving—not under any compulsion, but coming to our own convictions in our own hearts. And then following through on them.

7. What will be the end result of such giving (v 11, 12, 14, 15)? God will be praised, and the bonds of fellowship between Christians living in different areas will be strengthened. There is a kind of virtuous circle in evidence here. God gives us grace. We are generous to other Christians, they in turn are grateful for us, and they give thanks to God.

8. Giving, according to Paul, is both good for us and promotes God's glory. How do these two work together? The basic principle is laid out in verse 6: whoever sows sparingly will also reap sparingly, and whoever sows generously will also reap bountifully. This is what lies behind the obligation-free, pain-free opportunity to share resources in verse 7, as we are encouraged to give thoughtfully—neither reluctantly nor under compulsion. God loves a cheerful giver. We tend to believe that God gives credit to a reluctant but careful giver. Paul seems to have something a little freer, a little more lavish in mind! When it comes to giving, extravagance is good!

9. APPLY: How can we be a bit more "reckless" in our own giving? Give some practical examples. We need to be a bit more reckless in our giving, and to be joyful about it as we do. Metaphorically dancing our way up to the front with a broad smile on our faces every time we have the opportunity to give. And when we can't give, let's make sure we see it as missing out! If we're sad, it shouldn't be because

we've had to part with our hard-earned pennies, but because, by not giving, we have missed out on great joy from God!

10. APPLY: How can we encourage each other to be more generous with what God has given to us, and encourage a spirit of generosity in our churches? Cultures differ, but many people are reticent about talking about their wealth and earnings and giving. We need to cultivate an atmosphere where we are more relaxed in talking about money in a godly way, and in encouraging each other to be generous.

2 Corinthians 10 – 11
THE BOASTING APOSTLE

THE BIG IDEA
The message as delivered by and through the apostles is the one true gospel that can save us. We must commit to it, and to those leaders who teach and live it. These are the leaders who truly love us.

SUMMARY
These are two very difficult chapters in this letter. Paul has laid out the way of true discipleship and ministry, and shown how the gospel impacts all of life, including our finances. It appears that the Corinthians have moved a little towards regarding Paul as someone who has the authority of an apostle, but they are still wavering. They thought Paul was unimpressive as a teacher, and much preferred the ministry of "super-apostles" who talked up their big credentials, had impressive oratory and spiritual experiences to talk about. Paul

knows that the qualifications for his ministry are Christ's calling, his humility and utter devotion to those he is seeking to serve. So, with tongue firmly wedged in cheek, he does something that completely goes against the grain for him. He parodies the boasting of the super-apostles, and talks about how he is way more qualified to be their teacher, leader and apostle than the false teachers are. He clearly hates doing this, but feels compelled to do so in order to press the point home that they are false teachers, and that he is the real deal.

He makes it clear that this is a spiritual battle, and that, ultimately, these teachers are not Christian at all, but agents of the devil. He reiterates his religious pedigree in 11:21-22. And then he talks about the amount he has endangered himself and suffered for the gospel and for themselves.

OPTIONAL EXTRA

Play a game of false boasting. Get the first person in the group to make a small boast about something they did: "I won the 100m race when I was 11 at school". The next person has to make a bigger claim and so on around the group "I won the school record for the 400m when I was 14". Anyone can shout "Cheat" at any time, and the person who made the claim has to admit if it is true or false. Just a bit of fun, but it introduces some important themes for the study.

GUIDANCE FOR QUESTIONS

1. How do people react when they are verbally attacked or criticised? People can get angry, defensive, or curl up in a ball and or hide. Often these kinds of criticism can also badly affect those who love us as well.

- **How do you react?** A chance for people to share something of their own experience and reactions to criticism.

2. By implication, what criticisms were being made about Paul in verses 11:6, 7, 8 (see also 10:1, 7)? They thought that Paul was timid, and was not of impressive appearance. His natural humility was taken as a sign of his lack of authority. He was not a trained speaker, and did not ask for money. Paul made it a principle not to be a financial burden to the Corinthians, by working with his own hands, or being supported by other churches. But these principles were turned against him as "proof" that he was not a true apostle.

- **What does he say the "super-apostles really are? What is their motivation and intention?** They are false and deceitful teachers who are pretending to be angels of light, but they are really the servants of Satan, trying to trick, deceive and compromise God's people.

- **What will become of them in the end (v 15)?** Paul alludes to the fact that they will be judged most severely for their lies.

4. How do we spot a false teacher, according to Paul? By their message (see 4:2)—their gospel is different to the one delivered by Paul. They also commend themselves, and boast about their exploits and achievements. Their teaching will usually appeal to our pride.

5. APPLY: False teachers are still prevalent in our world. How can we spot them, and how can we resist their pull? We need to know the gospel clearly and thoroughly, so that we will spot when someone diverges from it. We should not be impressed by people who are "impressive"—good speakers, who tell funny stories and make us feel emotional. 2 Corinthians 4 tells us that true gospel ministers will reject underhand manipulative ways, and will always be prepared to give a plain statement of the truth of the gospel.

6. What has the life of Paul the apostle been like? Why does he list the physical dangers he has been in? He is not appealing for sympathy or boasting about these difficulties to make himself seem great. He is doing so to underline how God has been with him, helped him to persevere and protected him through "many a danger, toil and snare" (a line from Amazing Grace).

7. What are the greater burdens he bears (v 28-29)? His anxiety for the churches he serves. He feels intensely for them and their problems and trials. So much so that his emotions run in parallel with theirs.

- **Why are these more difficult than the physical danger he has been in?** He can bear physical hardship, because he is happy to spend himself for the sake of Christ. But his worry and concern for the Corinthians is what keeps him up at night.

8. What would Paul much rather boast about and why (v 30)? He wants to boast about the things that show his weakness, not his strength—so that Christ is glorified, not him

• **What is the big principle here that he wants them to understand?** Weakness is the sign of greatness. It is only as we are weak that God's greatness and goodness shines through us. When we are weak he is strong, and he receives the glory for what we do. We hold this treasure in cracked vessels as Paul has said in 4:7. Any

boasting about strength or prowess is out of place, and is only a sign that someone is a false teacher.

9. APPLY: What do you think success is as a Christian? How will you need to think differently about that now? Success is not about personal achievement. It is about faithfulness and celebrating God's work in and through you as you show his greatness through your weakness.

10. APPLY: What is going to be different this week as a result of what you have seen in this passage? Allow the group to speak honestly, and don't neglect to pray for people as they seek to re-orientate their lives around the gospel message.

7 2 Corinthians 12 – 13
VISIONS AND VALUES

THE BIG IDEA
Paul starts his final plea for the Corinthians to repent and set things straight in their lives and in their relationship with him as a genuine apostle before he comes to them in judgment. He compares his ministry and life with the other teachers that the Corinthians thought were much more impressive than him.

SUMMARY
As this long and complex letter comes to a close, Paul starts to sum up all that he has taught them. The Corinthians are obsessed with the impressive credentials, powerful speaking and compelling experiences of the false teachers. Paul by comparison seems

weak, ineffectual and unimpressive. Paul has been showing them repeatedly through this letter that weakness is the way of the cross, and therefore the way of the Christian life.

Much against his better judgement, Paul "boasts" in a self-deprecating and ironic way about all the things that have happened to him that establish his credentials as a true servant of Christ and the gospel message. The false teachers boast about their successes, wealth and fame. Paul boasts about his beatings, sufferings and weakness. These, he says are the true marks of a follower of Christ.

Paul lays down an ultimatum with the authority he has as an apostle of Christ.

He is calling on those in the Corinthian congregation to repent and change their ways. What will happen is not specified, but there is a suggestion that Paul will wield his authority in judgment upon them. On previous visits, he has taught and warned. He has prayed for them, argued with them and urged them from afar with his letters, and through the representations of Titus and others he has sent. But the threat to them is now real (see 13:10).

Paul is motivated, not by money, or the fame he may get from the support of the Corinthian church, but genuine love for them. He knows that what is best for them is to live by the true gospel of Christ, and to apply it to every area of their lives. So he concludes (13:5-14) by appealing to them to repent, before he has to come in judgment.

The final encouragements and greetings (13:11-14) are an appeal to be restored: to God and the gospel; to himself as a true apostle; and to one another.

OPTIONAL EXTRA

Have a brief game of "Would you rather, where group members have to choose between two difficult alternatives. Some ideas can be found here: conversationstartersworld.com/would-you-rather-questions/

GUIDANCE FOR QUESTIONS

1. What has been your experience of good Christian leaders? What is it about them that you appreciated? Try to avoid talking about your current leaders, and make sure that you draw out the difference between a "talented" leader (good preacher, fun to be with, musical), and someone with good Christian leadership qualities (loving, thoughtful, prayerful, faithful).

• **What has been your experience of poor Christian leaders? Where did they go wrong, do you think?** Again, avoid discussion of current leaders—try to draw out some of the poor personal qualities they displayed—arrogance, not listening well, an inability to consult in decision making, wobbly theology, etc. Try to talk about ways that they were perhaps not supported or encouraged by the congregation, as well as deficiencies in their training and practice.

2. Why does Paul start to "boast" about his spiritual experience in verses 1-4? The false teachers in Corinth clearly talked openly about the special revelations and visions they had in order to make themselves sound superior and impressive. Paul talks about his experience for a very different reason.

• **What effect might this experience have had upon him (v 7)?** He is clearly embarrassed about having to talk about this experience, which is very private and personal to him. This is why he puts the reporting of it in the third person. But Paul knows that he may easily have become conceited with the knowledge he had been given.

3. Why did God give Paul a "thorn in the flesh"? In passing, Paul makes the point that if anyone is going to judge him, or anyone else for that matter, they should do it on the basis of what they see or hear, not what experiences they may or may not have had. Paul's own experiences could match— or even outstrip—anything they could lay claim to. But for Paul, any advantage that flowed from this great privilege was that it led to a deeper experience of weakness. God gave him this "thorn in the flesh" so that he might not become big headed.

• **Why did God not take it away from him when Paul asked?** Again, Paul holds back the details—he doesn't tell us whether this was mental illness, bad eyesight, a poor marriage, or something completely different, like the opposition he routinely faced around the Mediterranean—because that's not the point. The point is that God acted (by giving Satan permission) to torment him—why? So that Paul would hear God say, "My grace is sufficient for you, for my power is made perfect in weakness" (v 9) and that Paul himself would learn to live out the principle of verses 9-10.

4. How does Paul summarise his views on strength, weakness and his suffering in the service of the gospel? This takes us right to the heart of what it means to be a Christian. This is real wisdom—to boast in our sufferings, in our disgrace, in our weakness. This is the wisdom of the cross. This is where we find grace. This is where we find strength. This is why there is so much riding on this that it is worth "playing the fool" in these chapters, in order that these people whom he loves so deeply will rediscover the wisdom of God. This is the wisdom he wrote about at the start of his first letter (see 1 Corinthians 1:20-31)—the wisdom that is found in the cross of Christ, our suffering Saviour. We find forgiveness and new life through the suffering of Christ. The road to glory is through suffering.

5. APPLY: What do Paul's experiences teach us about the highs and lows of our lives as Christians? It is clear that Paul has never spoken about his spiritual experience before, and can hardly bring himself to describe it now—and will certainly not reveal the content of it. These things can come to us as gifts from God, but they are also dangerous—they can lead to conceit. So we must treat our own experiences, and those that others report to us in books or in talks with great care.

• **Why is it so hard to embrace—let alone boast about—our weakness? What will bring us to the point that Paul reaches in verse 10?** We are proud and stubborn people, and our culture views health and illness, strength and weakness, boasting and humility, as opposite ends of a spectrum. Paul has learned to see that all things come from God, and rather than to be avoided, these things must be embraced. The gospel of Christ shows us a new way to view them. Weakness is not bad, the very opposite, in fact. It is only in and through the "weakness" of Christ on the cross that salvation has been won. And it is only when we are weak, that the glory of the gospel can shine through us.

6. Paul is preparing to visit the Corinthians again. What warnings does he give the church (v 1-3)? Paul lays down an ultimatum with the authority he has as an apostle of Christ. He is calling on those in the Corinthian congregation to repent and change their ways. What will happen is not specified, but there is a suggestion that Paul will wield his authority in judgment upon them.

• **What will happen if they ignore the warnings and continue in their false ways?** On previous visits, he has taught and warned. Absent from them he has prayed for them and argued with them and urged them from afar with his letters, and through the representations of Titus and others he has sent. But the threat to them is now real (see 13:10).

7. What does Paul say they must do before he arrives (v 5)? They must examine themselves and then test themselves to see if their faith is genuine—faith based on the gospel of glory through suffering, of wisdom through the foolishness of the cross.

• **What is his ultimate aim and motivation for saying this (v 7-10)?** He is wanting them to be restored—in their relationship with Christ and in their relationship with himself. His motivation is not rivalry or jealousy, but love. He is praying for them, and does not mind if he suffers, so long as they are truly strong in the truth of the gospel.

8. How do Paul's final greetings and prayer (v 11-14) sum up what he longs to happen in the Corinthian church? Paul is so committed to these half-hearted, confused believers—who, let's remember had no doubt hurt him deeply by believing all kinds of lies and slander about him—but he is still so committed to them that he will not stop pursuing them—and in fact says that he will most gladly spend and be spent for their souls. He will pour himself out for them. The irony is, of course, that according to 12:15, they were so mixed up that as his love for them increased, theirs for him seemed to decrease—but not even that deterred Paul. He still pursues the Corinthians, because he loves them.

9. APPLY: All of us are more than capable of being selfish in relationships. What can motivate us to stick with difficult people as Paul did? What produces this kind of love for people? This willingness to stick with them, put up with them, pursue them at such real personal cost? Only one thing can do that to a human being, and that is the discovery that we have first been pursued by another. Paul had experienced that personally, when the same Jesus Christ whom he hated and whose followers he had hounded, calmly caught up with him on the road to Damascus. And the end of one pursuit gave rise to the beginning of another, as Paul set out to be all things to all men in order that he might save some.

• **If love builds, what is our primary responsibility to one another? How do you think we might do this?** We must strive to live in true gospel fellowship. On one level this means challenging and urging each other to live according to the gospel of Christ in every area of life. But it also means comforting each other in our trials and struggles and failures, striving to live in peace with one another, and genuinely loving each other as Christ loved us.

10. APPLY: For Paul, loving the Corinthians meant challenging them to be godly. How does this fit with your understanding of love? Love pursues other people, and does not leave people to rot in their own mistakes and errors. Love actively seeks the higher good of other people. We know that the best thing for people is to live according to God's ways, and in the light of the truth of the gospel. That is what we will be committed to.

• **How does Paul's love for the Corinthians express itself in his prayers for them?** What is the most loving thing we can pray for other people? That they know and live by the truth of the gospel and do not get knocked off-track by false teaching, false spirituality, false ideas of what "success" means in the Christian life. And that they live out the gospel in their attitudes to money, fellowship and every aspect of Christian living.

EXPLORE MORE

Take a moment to write down three key things that you have learned from 2 Corinthians about God, the gospel and the Christian life. Encourage the group to apply the lessons about the marks of true leadership and genuine gospel application to their lives. Weakness is to be embraced as the pattern of how God works in our lives. **Now write down three things that**

God has challenged you to think and do differently in the power which he supplies in Christ through the Spirit. Make sure that the group applies the gospel to all areas of their lives—including their attitude to money—and do not neglect to see how this is both personal, and also corporate—for our lives as a fellowship together, as well as for us as individuals.

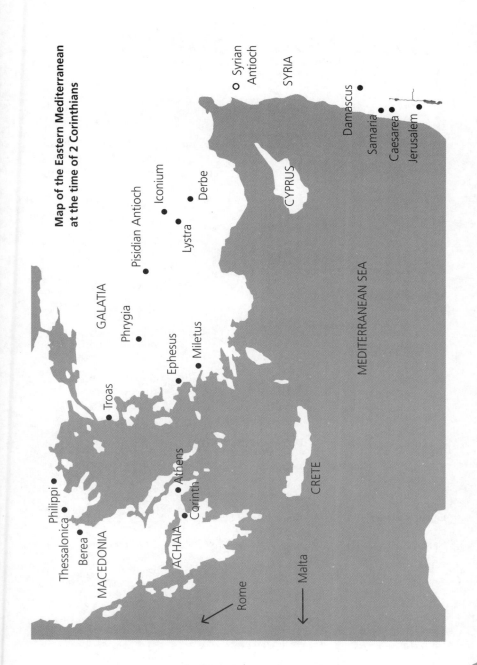

Map of the Eastern Mediterranean at the time of 2 Corinthians

Good Book Guides
The full range

Galatians: 7 Studies
Timothy Keller
ISBN: 9781908762566

Ephesians: 10 Studies
Thabiti Anyabwile
ISBN: 9781907377099

Ephesians: 8 Studies
Richard Coekin
ISBN: 9781910307694

Philippians: 7 Studies
Steven J. Lawson
ISBN: 9781784981181

Colossians: 6 Studies
Mark Meynell
ISBN: 9781906334246

1 Thessalonians:
7 Studies
Mark Wallace
ISBN: 9781904889533

1&2 Timothy: 7 Studies
Phillip Jensen
ISBN: 9781784980191

Titus: 5 Studies
Tim Chester
ISBN: 9781909919631

Hebrews: 8 Studies
Justin Buzzard
ISBN: 9781906334420

James: 6 Studies
Sam Allberry
ISBN: 9781910307816

1 Peter: 6 Studies
Juan R. Sanchez
ISBN: 9781784980177

1 John: 7 Studies
Nathan Buttery
ISBN: 9781904889953

Revelation: 7 Studies
Tim Chester
ISBN: 9781910307021

TOPICAL

Man of God: 10 Studies
Anthony Bewes & Sam Allberry
ISBN: 9781904889977

Biblical Womanhood:
10 Studies
Sarah Collins
ISBN: 9781907377532

The Apostles' Creed:
10 Studies
Tim Chester
ISBN: 9781905564415

Promises Kept: Bible Overview: 9 Studies
Carl Laferton
ISBN: 9781908317933

The Reformation Solas
6 Studies
Jason Helopoulos
ISBN: 9781784981501

Contentment: 6 Studies
Anne Woodcock
ISBN: 9781905564668

Women of Faith:
8 Studies
Mary Davis
ISBN: 9781904889526

Meeting Jesus: 8 Studies
Jenna Kavonic
ISBN: 9781905564460

Heaven: 6 Studies
Andy Telfer
ISBN: 9781909919457

Making Work Work:
8 Studies
Marcus Nodder
ISBN: 9781908762894

The Holy Spirit: 8 Studies
Pete & Anne Woodcock
ISBN: 9781905564217

Experiencing God:
6 Studies
Tim Chester
ISBN: 9781906334437

Real Prayer: 7 Studies
Anne Woodcock
ISBN: 9781910307595

thegoodbook
COMPANY

BIBLICAL | RELEVANT | ACCESSIBLE

At The Good Book Company, we are dedicated to helping Christians and local churches grow. We believe that God's growth process always starts with hearing clearly what he has said to us through his timeless word—the Bible.

Ever since we opened our doors in 1991, we have been striving to produce Bible-based resources that bring glory to God. We have grown to become an international provider of user-friendly resources to the Christian community, with believers of all backgrounds and denominations using our books, Bible studies, devotionals, evangelistic resources, and DVD-based courses.

We want to equip ordinary Christians to live for Christ day by day, and churches to grow in their knowledge of God, their love for one another, and the effectiveness of their outreach.

Call us for a discussion of your needs or visit one of our local websites for more information on the resources and services we provide.

Your friends at The Good Book Company

thegoodbook.com | thegoodbook.co.uk
thegoodbook.com.au | thegoodbook.co.nz
thegoodbook.co.in